Sunlight

by Erin Edison
Consulting Editor: Gail Saunders-Smith, PhD

CAPSTONE PRESS
a capstone imprint

Pebble Plus is published by Capstone Press,
1710 Roe Crest Drive, North Mankato, Minnesota 56003.
www.capstonepub.com

Copyright © 2012 by Capstone Press, a Capstone imprint. All rights reserved.
No part of this publication may be reproduced in whole or in part, or stored in a retrieval system, or transmitted in any form or by any means, electronic, mechanical, photocopying, recording, or otherwise, without written permission of the publisher. For information regarding permission, write to Capstone Press,
1710 Roe Crest Drive, North Mankato, Minnesota 56003.

Library of Congress Cataloging-in-Publication Data
Edison, Erin.
 Sunlight / by Erin Edison.
  p. cm.—(Pebble plus. Weather basics)
 Summary: "Simple text and full-color photographs describe sunlight and how it causes temperature changes, the seasons, wind, and clouds"—Provided by publisher.
 Includes bibliographical references and index.
 ISBN 978-1-4296-6056-3 (library binding)
 ISBN 978-1-4296-7081-4 (paperback)
 ISBN 978-1-4296-8753-9 (saddle-stitch)
 1. Sunshine—Juvenile literature. 2. Sun—Temperature—Juvenile literature. I. Title. II. Series.
 QC911.2.E35 2012
 551.5'271—dc22   2010053942

Editorial Credits
Erika L. Shores, editor; Kyle Grenz, designer; Laura Manthe, production specialist

Photo Credits
Alamy: PSL Images/NASA, 11, PVstock.com, 7; Dreamstime: Afhunta, 15, Alexstar, 12, 14, Optimist79, 21, Pozn, back cover; Getty Images Inc.: Taxi/Barbara Peacock, 17; PhotoEdit Inc.: James Shaffer, 19; Shutterstock: Andriano, cover, djgis, 1, Efired, 9, Peter Sobolev, 13, Vibrant Image Studio, 5

Artistic Effects
Shutterstock: marcus55

Capstone Press thanks Mike Shores, earth science teacher at RBA Public Charter School in Mankato, Minnesota, for his assistance on this book.

Note to Parents and Teachers

The Weather Basics series supports national science standards related to earth science. This book describes and illustrates sunlight. The images support early readers in understanding the text. The repetition of words and phrases helps early readers learn new words. This book also introduces early readers to subject-specific vocabulary words, which are defined in the Glossary section. Early readers may need assistance to read some words and to use the Table of Contents, Glossary, Read More, Internet Sites, and Index sections of the book.

Table of Contents

Sunlight 4
Day and Night 10
Sun and Earth 12
We Need the Sun . . . 20

Glossary 22
Read More 23
Internet Sites 23
Index 24

Sunlight

Sunlight comes right from the sun. It gives Earth light and heat. It makes Earth's weather.

Sunlight travels in rays. The rays heat Earth's atmosphere unevenly. It causes pockets of cool and warm air. These air pockets move and cause wind.

Sunlight heats bodies of water. The heat causes water to evaporate into the air. Clouds form and carry water around Earth.

Day and Night

The sun lights half of Earth at a time. When it's day on one side, it's night on the other. As Earth spins, places move in and out of light.

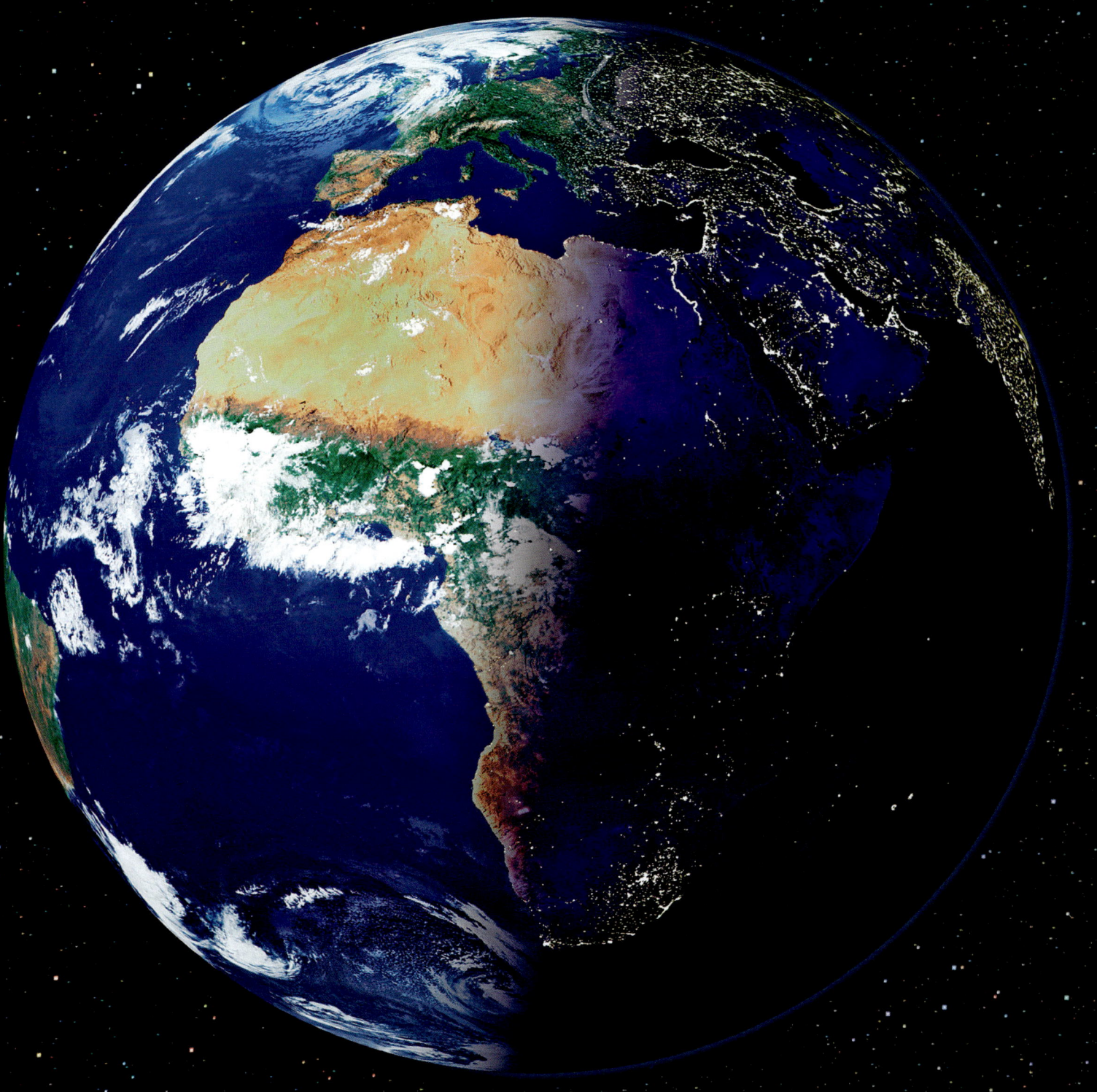

Sun and Earth

Sunlight is strongest at places near the equator. The sun shines directly down on this area. All the sunlight makes the air hot.

equator

The sun's rays hit Earth's poles at an angle. The weak sunlight doesn't warm the air as much. Ice and snow cover the poles all year.

North Pole

South Pole

In June, Earth's top half is tilted toward the sun. It's summer here. Earth's bottom half gets less sun. It's winter there.

In December, the top of Earth is tilted away from the sun. It's winter here. More sunlight hits the bottom half of Earth. It's summer there.

We Need the Sun

Plants wouldn't grow without sunlight. Animals wouldn't have food. Without the sun's heat, oceans would freeze. Sunlight makes life on Earth possible.

Glossary

atmosphere—the mixture of gases that surrounds Earth

equator—an imaginary line around the middle of Earth

evaporate—the action of a liquid changing into a gas; heat causes water to evaporate

pole—the top or bottom part of a planet

ray—a line of light that beams out from the sun

tilt—angle or leaning; not straight

Read More

Barraclough, Sue. *Sunlight.* Investigate. Chicago: Heinemann Library, 2008.

Purdie, Kate. *Sunshine and Drought.* Weatherwise. New York: PowerKids Press, 2010.

Internet Sites

FactHound offers a safe, fun way to find Internet sites related to this book. All of the sites on FactHound have been researched by our staff.

Here's all you do:

Visit *www.facthound.com*

Type in this code: 9781429660563

Check out projects, games and lots more at
www.capstonekids.com

Index

animals, 20
atmosphere, 6
clouds, 8
day, 10
equator, 12
evaporation, 8
heat, 4, 6, 8, 12, 14, 20
night, 10
oceans, 20

plants, 20
poles, 14
rays, 6, 14
summer, 16, 18
water, 8
weather, 4
wind, 6
winter, 16, 18

Word Count: 211
Grade: 1
Early-Intervention Level: 17